Cyber Attacks In American Hospitals

Story Of Cyber Threats, Protecting Patient Care, and Building a Resilient Healthcare System In The United States

Steve Sigurdson

Copyright © 2024 Steve Sigurdson

All rights reserved. No part of this publication may be reproduced, distributed, or transmitted in any form or by any means, including photocopying, recording, or other electronic or mechanical methods, without the prior written permission of the publisher, except in the case of brief quotations embodied in critical reviews and certain other noncommercial uses permitted by copyright law

Table Of Contents

Introduction

Chapter 1

Understanding Cyber Threats in Healthcare

Chapter 2

Assessing Vulnerabilities in Healthcare Systems

Chapter 3

Compliance Requirements and Regulatory Frameworks

Chapter 4

Strategies for Healthcare Cyber Defense

Chapter 5

The Future of Healthcare Cybersecurity

Conclusion

INTRODUCTION

Introduction

In an increasingly digitalized healthcare landscape, the importance of cybersecurity cannot be overstated. As healthcare organizations adopt advanced technologies to improve patient care, streamline operations, and enhance efficiency, they also become prime targets for cybercriminals seeking to exploit vulnerabilities and compromise critical systems and data. This introduction explores the significance of healthcare cybersecurity and provides an overview of the cyber threats facing the healthcare sector.

Healthcare cybersecurity is not merely a matter of protecting sensitive data; it is a matter of safeguarding patient care, privacy, and trust. Patient health information (PHI) is among the most valuable and sensitive data assets, containing personal, medical, and financial information that must be protected against unauthorized access, use, or disclosure. A breach of patient data not only violates privacy rights but also jeopardizes patient safety, undermines trust in healthcare providers, and can have far-reaching consequences for individuals, organizations, and communities.

Moreover, the healthcare sector is increasingly reliant on interconnected digital technologies, including electronic health records (EHRs), medical devices, telehealth platforms, and Internet-of-Things (IoT) devices, to deliver care and support organizational operations. While these technologies offer unprecedented opportunities for improving diagnosis, treatment, and patient outcomes, they also introduce new risks and challenges that must be addressed proactively. From ransomware attacks and data breaches to insider threats and supply chain risks, the cybersecurity threats facing the healthcare sector are diverse, complex, and ever-evolving.

The healthcare sector faces a myriad of cyber threats, each posing unique risks and challenges to patient care, confidentiality, and organizational resilience. One of the most prevalent threats facing healthcare organizations is ransomware, a type of malicious software designed to encrypt data and demand payment for its release. Ransomware attacks can disrupt critical operations, compromise patient data, and cause significant financial and reputational damage to affected organizations. Moreover, ransomware attacks targeting healthcare providers have become increasingly frequent and sophisticated, with cybercriminals exploiting vulnerabilities in legacy systems, remote access tools, and third-party software to gain unauthorized access to healthcare networks.

In addition to ransomware, healthcare organizations must contend with data breaches, phishing scams, insider threats, and supply chain risks, among other cyber threats. Data breaches involving the theft or unauthorized access of patient data can have devastating consequences for individuals and organizations, including identity theft, financial fraud, and legal liabilities. Phishing scams, which involve tricking individuals into revealing sensitive information or downloading malware, pose a significant risk to healthcare organizations, as employees may inadvertently disclose credentials or click on malicious links, leading to data breaches or system compromise.

Furthermore, insider threats, whether malicious or inadvertent, can pose significant challenges for healthcare organizations, as employees, contractors, or trusted insiders with access to sensitive data may abuse their privileges or mishandle information, leading to data breaches, privacy violations, or compliance issues. Similarly, supply chain risks stemming from third-party vendors, suppliers, and service providers can introduce vulnerabilities that can be exploited by cybercriminals to gain unauthorized access to healthcare networks or compromise critical systems or data.

Healthcare cybersecurity is essential for protecting patient care, privacy, and trust in an increasingly digitalized healthcare environment. By understanding the cyber threats facing the healthcare sector and implementing robust cybersecurity measures and best practices, healthcare organizations can enhance their resilience to cyber threats and ensure the continuity of critical services for patients and communities alike.

Chapter 1: Understanding Cyber Threats in Healthcare

Cyber threats pose significant risks to the healthcare sector, threatening patient care, privacy, and organizational resilience. Understanding the nature of these threats is essential for healthcare organizations to develop effective cybersecurity strategies and mitigate the impact of cyberattacks.

Healthcare organizations are vulnerable to a wide range of cyberattacks, each with its own tactics, motivations, and consequences. One of the most prevalent types of cyberattacks targeting healthcare organizations is ransomware. Ransomware attacks involve malicious software that encrypts data and demands payment for its release. These attacks can disrupt critical operations, compromise patient data, and cause financial and reputational damage. Healthcare providers are particularly attractive targets for ransomware attacks due to the sensitive nature of patient data and the criticality of healthcare services.

In addition to ransomware, healthcare organizations face threats from data breaches, phishing scams, insider threats, and supply chain attacks. Data breaches involve the unauthorized access or theft of sensitive information, such as patient records or financial data. Phishing scams target employees with deceptive emails or messages designed to trick them into revealing sensitive information or downloading malware. Insider threats, whether intentional or unintentional, can result in the misuse or mishandling of sensitive data by employees or trusted insiders. Supply chain attacks exploit vulnerabilities in third-party vendors or service providers to gain unauthorized access to healthcare networks or systems.

Cybercriminals employ a variety of tactics, techniques, and procedures (TTPs) to target healthcare organizations and exploit vulnerabilities in their systems and networks. These TTPs may include:

- Social engineering: Cybercriminals use social engineering techniques, such as phishing emails or pretexting, to trick employees into revealing sensitive information or granting access to systems.

- Malware: Malicious software, such as ransomware, viruses, or trojans, is used to infect healthcare systems and encrypt data, disrupt operations, or steal sensitive information.
- Exploiting vulnerabilities: Cybercriminals exploit known vulnerabilities in software, applications, or networks to gain unauthorized access or execute malicious activities.
- Credential theft: Cybercriminals steal login credentials or passwords through various means, such as phishing scams or brute force attacks, to gain unauthorized access to healthcare systems or networks.
- Insider threats: Insiders with legitimate access to healthcare systems may abuse their privileges or intentionally compromise data for personal gain or malicious purposes.

By understanding these TTPs, healthcare organizations can better identify and defend against cyber threats, implement effective security controls, and respond promptly to incidents.

Numerous healthcare organizations have fallen victim to cyberattacks in recent years, highlighting the severity and impact of cyber threats on patient care and organizational operations. One notable example is the WannaCry ransomware attack in 2017, which affected healthcare organizations worldwide, including the National Health Service (NHS) in the United Kingdom. The attack disrupted healthcare services, delayed patient appointments and surgeries, and compromised patient data, underscoring the importance of cybersecurity in healthcare.

Another significant cyberattack targeted Anthem Inc., one of the largest health insurance companies in the United States, in 2015. The breach compromised the personal and medical information of approximately 78.8 million individuals, including names, social security numbers, dates of birth, and medical IDs. The incident resulted in regulatory fines, legal settlements, and reputational damage for Anthem, highlighting the financial and legal consequences of cybersecurity breaches in healthcare.

Similarly, the NotPetya ransomware attack in 2017 disrupted operations at numerous healthcare organizations worldwide, including hospitals and pharmaceutical companies. The attack encrypted data, disrupted critical systems, and caused widespread chaos and disruption, emphasizing the importance of robust cybersecurity defenses and incident response capabilities.

These case studies illustrate the severity and impact of cyberattacks on healthcare organizations and underscore the need for proactive cybersecurity measures, risk management strategies, and incident response planning to protect patient care and organizational resilience. By learning from past incidents and implementing effective security controls, healthcare organizations can mitigate the risk of cyber threats and safeguard patient data and safety.

Chapter 2: Assessing Vulnerabilities in Healthcare Systems

Healthcare systems are complex ecosystems that rely heavily on technology to deliver patient care and manage operations. However, this reliance on technology also introduces vulnerabilities that can be exploited by cyber attackers. Assessing these vulnerabilities is essential for healthcare organizations to identify weaknesses, prioritize security measures, and mitigate risks effectively.

Healthcare systems often consist of a mix of legacy and modern technologies, creating a diverse and sometimes fragmented infrastructure. Legacy systems, in particular, may lack robust security features and receive limited support or updates from vendors, making them vulnerable to exploitation. Furthermore, complex networks and interconnected systems increase the attack surface and create opportunities for cyber attackers to infiltrate healthcare networks.

In addition to infrastructure vulnerabilities, healthcare organizations must assess weaknesses in processes and security measures. Inadequate access controls, weak authentication mechanisms, and insufficient encryption protocols can leave sensitive data exposed to unauthorized access or theft. Similarly, gaps in patch management, software updates, and system configurations can create opportunities for cyber attackers to exploit known vulnerabilities and gain access to healthcare systems.

Moreover, third-party vendors and service providers introduce additional risks to healthcare organizations. Supply chain risks, such as vulnerabilities in software or hardware components supplied by third parties, can expose healthcare systems to cyber threats. Similarly, outsourcing certain functions, such as IT support or medical device maintenance, may introduce security vulnerabilities if proper security controls and oversight are not in place.

Insider threats pose significant challenges for healthcare organizations, as employees, contractors, or trusted insiders with access to sensitive data may intentionally or inadvertently compromise security. Malicious insiders may abuse their privileges to steal data, sabotage systems, or disrupt operations for personal gain or malicious purposes. Similarly, negligent or unaware insiders may inadvertently mishandle data, fall victim to social engineering attacks, or violate security policies, leading to data breaches or system compromise.

Supply chain risks represent another significant vulnerability for healthcare organizations, as third-party vendors and service providers may introduce security vulnerabilities into healthcare systems. Vulnerabilities in software or hardware components supplied by third parties can be exploited by cyber attackers to gain unauthorized access to healthcare networks or compromise critical systems or data. Healthcare organizations must conduct thorough due diligence on vendors and service providers, assess their security practices, and implement contractual agreements and security controls to mitigate supply chain risks effectively.

Legacy systems present unique challenges for healthcare organizations, as these outdated technologies may lack robust security features and receive limited support or updates from vendors. Vulnerabilities in legacy systems can be exploited by cyber attackers to gain unauthorized access to healthcare networks, compromise patient data, or disrupt critical operations. Healthcare organizations must prioritize the modernization of legacy systems, implement compensating security controls, and monitor for signs of compromise to mitigate the risks associated with legacy technologies effectively.

While technological vulnerabilities are a significant concern, the human factor remains one of the most significant challenges for healthcare cybersecurity. Employees, including clinicians, administrative staff, and IT professionals, play a critical role in safeguarding patient data and protecting healthcare systems from cyber threats. However, human error, negligence, and lack of awareness can undermine security efforts and increase the risk of data breaches and security incidents.

Education and training are essential for empowering healthcare employees to recognize and respond to cyber threats effectively. Healthcare organizations must provide comprehensive cybersecurity training programs that cover topics such as phishing awareness, password hygiene, data handling procedures, and incident response protocols. By educating employees about common cyber threats, security best practices, and their role in protecting patient data, organizations can enhance security awareness, reduce the risk of security incidents, and foster a culture of cybersecurity throughout the organization.

Furthermore, healthcare organizations must implement robust access controls, authentication mechanisms, and user monitoring capabilities to prevent unauthorized access and detect suspicious activity. Role-based access controls ensure that employees have access to only the information and systems necessary to perform their job duties, reducing the risk of insider threats and unauthorized access. Similarly, multi-factor authentication (MFA) adds an extra layer of security by requiring users to provide multiple forms of identification before accessing sensitive data or systems.

Assessing vulnerabilities in healthcare systems is essential for identifying weaknesses, prioritizing security measures, and mitigating risks effectively. By identifying infrastructure vulnerabilities, addressing insider threats and supply chain risks, and educating and empowering healthcare employees, organizations can enhance their resilience to cyber threats and protect patient data and safety. A proactive approach to cybersecurity, combined with ongoing risk assessments and security awareness training, is essential for safeguarding the future of healthcare in an increasingly digitalized world.

Chapter 3: Compliance Requirements and Regulatory Frameworks

Compliance requirements and regulatory frameworks play a crucial role in shaping healthcare cybersecurity practices and standards. In an industry where patient data privacy and security are paramount, healthcare organizations must adhere to various regulations to ensure the protection of sensitive information and maintain compliance with legal and ethical standards. This section provides an overview of key healthcare regulations, examines compliance challenges and best practices, and discusses the delicate balance between security, privacy, and regulatory compliance.

Two of the most prominent regulations governing healthcare cybersecurity are the Health Insurance Portability and Accountability Act (HIPAA) in the United States and the General Data Protection Regulation (GDPR) in the European Union.

HIPAA, enacted in 1996, sets standards for the protection of sensitive patient health information (PHI) and establishes rules for healthcare providers, health plans, and healthcare clearinghouses to safeguard PHI. HIPAA includes provisions for ensuring the confidentiality, integrity, and availability of PHI, as well as requirements for conducting risk assessments, implementing security measures, and notifying individuals and regulatory authorities in the event of a data breach.

Similarly, GDPR, which came into effect in 2018, imposes strict requirements for the protection of personal data, including health data, and applies to organizations that process the personal data of EU residents. GDPR requires healthcare organizations to obtain explicit consent from individuals for the processing of their personal data, implement appropriate technical and organizational measures to ensure data security, and notify authorities and affected individuals in the event of a data breach.

Compliance with HIPAA and GDPR requires healthcare organizations to adopt comprehensive security measures, conduct regular risk assessments, and implement privacy controls to protect patient data and maintain regulatory compliance. Failure to comply with these regulations can result in severe penalties, including fines, legal liabilities, and reputational damage.

Achieving and maintaining compliance with healthcare regulations present numerous challenges for healthcare organizations. One of the primary challenges is the complexity and evolving nature of regulatory requirements, as healthcare regulations are subject to frequent updates and changes in response to emerging threats and technologies. Keeping up with these changes and ensuring ongoing compliance requires dedicated resources, expertise, and investment in cybersecurity infrastructure and capabilities.

Furthermore, healthcare organizations must navigate the complexities of data governance, data sharing, and data management in a highly regulated environment. Balancing the need for data access and interoperability with the requirements for data privacy and security poses challenges for healthcare organizations, particularly in the context of electronic health records (EHRs), health information exchange (HIE), and telemedicine.

Moreover, compliance with healthcare regulations requires collaboration and coordination across departments, stakeholders, and third-party vendors. Healthcare organizations must establish clear policies and procedures for managing

PHI, conducting risk assessments, and responding to security incidents, as well as provide ongoing training and education for employees to ensure compliance with regulatory requirements.

Despite these challenges, there are several best practices that healthcare organizations can implement to enhance compliance with healthcare regulations and improve cybersecurity posture:

1. Conduct regular risk assessments: Identify and prioritize security risks and vulnerabilities to patient data and healthcare systems, and develop mitigation strategies to address identified risks effectively.
2. Implement robust security controls: Implement technical, administrative, and physical security measures to protect patient

data, including encryption, access controls, and intrusion detection systems.

3. Train and educate employees: Provide comprehensive cybersecurity training and awareness programs for employees to recognize and respond to cyber threats effectively, including phishing scams, malware attacks, and social engineering tactics.

4. Monitor and audit compliance: Establish mechanisms for monitoring and auditing compliance with healthcare regulations, including regular security assessments, penetration testing, and compliance audits.

5. Engage with regulatory authorities: Maintain open communication and collaboration with regulatory authorities, industry organizations, and cybersecurity experts to stay informed about regulatory

updates, best practices, and emerging threats.

By implementing these best practices, healthcare organizations can strengthen their compliance efforts, mitigate security risks, and protect patient data from cyber threats effectively.

One of the key challenges for healthcare organizations is striking the right balance between security, privacy, and regulatory compliance. While regulatory requirements such as HIPAA and GDPR mandate specific security and privacy controls to protect patient data, organizations must also consider the broader ethical and legal implications of their cybersecurity practices. Balancing security, privacy, and regulatory compliance requires a multifaceted approach that considers the needs and expectations of patients, providers, regulators, and other stakeholders. Healthcare organizations must adopt a risk-based approach to cybersecurity that prioritizes the protection of sensitive data and critical systems while ensuring compliance with regulatory requirements and ethical standards.

Moreover, healthcare organizations must recognize that security and privacy are not mutually exclusive but rather complementary objectives that can be achieved through effective risk management and governance practices. By aligning security measures with privacy principles and regulatory requirements, healthcare organizations can enhance patient trust, minimize the risk of data breaches, and maintain compliance with healthcare regulations.

Compliance requirements and regulatory frameworks play a critical role in shaping healthcare cybersecurity practices and standards. By adhering to regulations such as HIPAA and GDPR, healthcare organizations can protect patient data, mitigate security risks, and maintain trust and confidence in the healthcare system. However, achieving and maintaining compliance requires ongoing effort, investment, and collaboration across departments, stakeholders, and regulatory authorities. By adopting best practices, implementing robust security controls, and striking the right balance between security, privacy, and regulatory compliance, healthcare organizations can enhance their resilience to cyber threats and safeguard patient data and safety in an increasingly digitalized healthcare environment.

Strategies for Healthcare Cyber Defense

Chapter 4: Strategies for Healthcare Cyber Defense

Ensuring robust cybersecurity defenses is paramount for healthcare organizations to protect patient data, maintain operational continuity, and safeguard the integrity of healthcare services. In an increasingly complex and evolving threat landscape, healthcare organizations must adopt comprehensive strategies for cyber defense that encompass proactive risk management, incident response planning, threat intelligence sharing, and technical controls and security measures.

Building resilience and incident response planning are foundational elements of effective cybersecurity defense for healthcare organizations. Resilience involves the ability to withstand and recover from cyberattacks, disruptions, or security incidents while maintaining critical services and minimizing the impact on patient care. Incident response planning encompasses the development of policies, procedures, and protocols for detecting, responding to, and recovering from cybersecurity incidents, including data breaches, malware infections, and system compromises.

Effective incident response planning begins with identifying and assessing potential threats and vulnerabilities to healthcare systems and data. Healthcare organizations must conduct comprehensive risk assessments to understand their cybersecurity posture, prioritize security measures, and develop incident response plans tailored to their unique risks and operational requirements. Incident response plans should outline roles and responsibilities, escalation procedures, communication protocols, and recovery strategies to facilitate a coordinated and effective response to security incidents.

Furthermore, healthcare organizations must conduct regular incident response drills, tabletop exercises, and simulations to test the effectiveness of their incident response plans and prepare staff for real-world security incidents. These exercises provide valuable opportunities for training and skill development, identify gaps or weaknesses in incident response procedures, and improve organizational readiness to respond to cyber threats effectively.

Threat intelligence sharing and collaboration are essential components of a proactive cybersecurity defense strategy for healthcare organizations. Threat intelligence involves the collection, analysis, and dissemination of information about cyber threats, vulnerabilities, and malicious actors to inform security decision-making and enhance threat detection and response capabilities.

Healthcare organizations can leverage threat intelligence from various sources, including government agencies, cybersecurity vendors, industry organizations, and information sharing platforms, to stay informed about emerging threats, trends, and best practices in cybersecurity. By participating in threat intelligence sharing initiatives and collaborative information sharing networks, healthcare organizations can access timely and relevant threat intelligence, share insights and experiences with peers, and collaborate with industry partners to improve cybersecurity defenses collectively.

Furthermore, threat intelligence sharing enables healthcare organizations to enhance their threat detection capabilities by integrating threat intelligence feeds into security monitoring tools and systems. By correlating threat intelligence with network and endpoint data, healthcare organizations can identify and respond to security threats more effectively, detect malicious activity early in the attack lifecycle, and mitigate the risk of data breaches and system compromises.

Implementing technical controls and security measures is essential for mitigating cybersecurity risks and protecting healthcare systems and data from unauthorized access, exploitation, and compromise. Technical controls encompass a wide range of security measures, including access controls, encryption, intrusion detection and prevention systems (IDPS), endpoint security solutions, and network segmentation, designed to prevent, detect, and mitigate security threats.

Access controls are fundamental to ensuring the confidentiality, integrity, and availability of healthcare data by limiting access to authorized users and resources based on predefined policies and permissions. Healthcare organizations must implement robust access controls, such as role-based access controls (RBAC), least privilege principles, and multi-factor authentication (MFA), to enforce access restrictions, prevent unauthorized access, and protect patient data from unauthorized disclosure or theft.

Encryption plays a critical role in safeguarding sensitive data against unauthorized access or disclosure by converting plaintext data into ciphertext using cryptographic algorithms. Healthcare organizations must implement encryption technologies to protect data at rest, in transit, and in use, including encryption of data stored on servers and storage devices, encryption of data transmitted over networks, and encryption of data processed by applications and databases.

Intrusion detection and prevention systems (IDPS) are essential for detecting and mitigating security threats in real-time by monitoring network traffic, identifying suspicious activity or anomalies, and taking proactive measures to block or mitigate potential threats. Healthcare organizations must deploy IDPS solutions to monitor network traffic, analyze security events, and detect and respond to security incidents effectively.

Endpoint security solutions are critical for protecting endpoints, such as desktops, laptops, and mobile devices, from malware, ransomware, and other security threats.

Healthcare organizations must implement endpoint security solutions, including antivirus software, endpoint detection and response (EDR) solutions, and mobile device management (MDM) platforms, to secure endpoints, prevent malware infections, and protect sensitive data from unauthorized access or theft.

Network segmentation involves dividing a network into multiple smaller, isolated segments to restrict the lateral movement of attackers and contain the impact of security incidents. Healthcare organizations must implement network segmentation techniques, such as virtual local area networks (VLANs), firewalls, and access control lists (ACLs), to segment networks, control traffic flow between segments, and minimize the risk of unauthorized access or data exfiltration.

Implementing technical controls and security measures is essential for mitigating cybersecurity risks and protecting healthcare systems and data from unauthorized access, exploitation, and compromise. By building resilience, developing incident response plans, leveraging threat intelligence sharing and collaboration, and implementing robust technical controls and security measures, healthcare organizations can enhance their cybersecurity defenses, mitigate security risks, and safeguard patient data and safety in an increasingly digitalized healthcare environment.

Chapter 5: The Future of Healthcare Cybersecurity

As healthcare systems continue to evolve and embrace digital technologies, the future of healthcare cybersecurity is fraught with both opportunities and challenges. Emerging trends and technologies in healthcare IT promise to revolutionize patient care and improve operational efficiency, but they also introduce new cybersecurity risks and vulnerabilities. This section explores the future of healthcare cybersecurity, including emerging trends and technologies, ethical considerations, privacy concerns, and patient rights, as well as strategies for safeguarding patients in an evolving threat landscape.

The future of healthcare cybersecurity is closely intertwined with emerging trends and technologies in healthcare IT, including artificial intelligence (AI), machine learning (ML), Internet of Things (IoT), telemedicine, and cloud computing. These technologies have the potential to transform patient care delivery, enhance clinical decision-making, and improve healthcare outcomes, but they also introduce new security challenges and risks.

Artificial intelligence and machine learning hold great promise for improving healthcare cybersecurity by enabling advanced threat detection, anomaly detection, and predictive analytics. AI and ML algorithms can analyze vast amounts of data to identify patterns, detect abnormalities, and predict potential security threats or vulnerabilities before they manifest into full-scale attacks. By leveraging AI-driven security solutions, healthcare organizations can enhance their threat detection capabilities, reduce false positives, and respond to security incidents more effectively.

The Internet of Things (IoT) presents both opportunities and challenges for healthcare cybersecurity. IoT devices, such as medical devices, wearable sensors, and remote monitoring systems, enable real-time data collection, remote patient monitoring, and personalized healthcare interventions. However, the proliferation of IoT devices also expands the attack surface and introduces new security vulnerabilities, such as insecure network connections, unpatched vulnerabilities, and insufficient authentication mechanisms. Healthcare organizations must implement robust security controls and protocols to secure IoT devices, protect patient data, and mitigate the risk of IoT-related cyber threats.

Telemedicine is another emerging trend in healthcare that is reshaping patient care delivery and access to healthcare services. Telemedicine enables patients to receive medical consultations, diagnoses, and treatment remotely via video conferencing, mobile apps, and other digital platforms. While telemedicine offers numerous benefits, such as improved access to care, reduced healthcare costs, and enhanced patient convenience, it also raises privacy and security concerns related to the transmission and storage of sensitive health information over digital networks. Healthcare organizations must implement encryption, access controls, and secure communication protocols to protect patient privacy and ensure the confidentiality of telemedicine sessions.

Cloud computing is revolutionizing healthcare IT infrastructure by providing scalable, flexible, and cost-effective solutions for storing, processing, and accessing healthcare data and applications. Cloud-based systems offer numerous benefits, including improved data accessibility, enhanced collaboration, and reduced IT infrastructure costs. However, cloud computing also introduces new security risks and challenges, such as data breaches, unauthorized access, and data loss.

Healthcare organizations must implement robust cloud security controls, such as encryption, identity and access management (IAM), and data loss prevention (DLP), to secure cloud-based systems and protect patient data from cyber threats.

As healthcare organizations adopt emerging technologies and digital solutions, it is essential to consider the ethical implications, privacy concerns, and patient rights associated with the collection, use, and sharing of healthcare data. Ethical considerations include issues related to patient consent, data ownership, data transparency, and data security. Healthcare organizations must obtain informed consent from patients for the collection, use, and sharing of their health information and ensure that patients understand how their data will be used and protected.

Privacy concerns arise from the increasing digitization and sharing of healthcare data, which can lead to unauthorized access, data breaches, and privacy violations. Healthcare organizations must implement robust privacy controls, such as encryption, access controls, and data anonymization, to protect patient privacy and comply with regulatory requirements, such as HIPAA and GDPR. Moreover, healthcare organizations must adopt a privacy-by-design approach that incorporates privacy principles and considerations into the design, development, and implementation of healthcare IT systems and applications.

Patient rights are central to the future of healthcare cybersecurity, as patients have the right to control their health information, access their medical records, and make informed decisions about their healthcare. Healthcare organizations must respect patient rights by implementing policies, procedures, and technologies that ensure patient autonomy, confidentiality, and consent. Patients should have the ability to access and manage their health information, request corrections to inaccuracies, and control who can access their data.

Looking ahead, safeguarding patients in an evolving threat landscape requires a holistic and proactive approach to healthcare cybersecurity that integrates technological solutions, policy frameworks, and ethical considerations. Healthcare organizations must invest in cybersecurity awareness and education programs to empower employees, patients, and stakeholders to recognize and respond to cyber threats effectively. Additionally, healthcare organizations must collaborate with industry partners, government agencies, and cybersecurity experts to share threat intelligence, best practices, and lessons learned to enhance collective cybersecurity defenses and mitigate emerging cyber threats.

Furthermore, healthcare organizations must adopt a risk-based approach to cybersecurity that prioritizes the protection of patient data and critical healthcare services while balancing security, privacy, and usability considerations. By conducting regular risk assessments, implementing robust security controls, and developing incident response plans, healthcare organizations can enhance their resilience to cyber threats and safeguard patient data and safety in an increasingly digitalized healthcare environment.

In conclusion, the future of healthcare cybersecurity is shaped by emerging trends and technologies, ethical considerations, privacy concerns, and patient rights. Healthcare organizations must embrace innovation while prioritizing security, privacy, and patient safety to address the evolving threat landscape effectively. By adopting a proactive and collaborative approach to cybersecurity, healthcare organizations can mitigate security risks, protect patient data, and ensure the integrity and trustworthiness of healthcare systems and services in the digital age.

Conclusion

In conclusion, the landscape of healthcare cybersecurity is rapidly evolving, presenting both opportunities and challenges for healthcare organizations worldwide. Throughout this exploration, several key findings and takeaways have emerged, shedding light on the complexities of securing patient data and healthcare systems in the digital age.

Healthcare organizations face a myriad of cybersecurity threats, ranging from ransomware attacks and data breaches to insider threats and supply chain risks. These threats not only jeopardize patient privacy and safety but also undermine the integrity and trustworthiness of healthcare services. It is imperative for healthcare organizations to adopt a proactive and holistic approach to cybersecurity that encompasses risk management, incident response planning, and collaboration with industry partners and regulatory authorities.

Emerging trends and technologies, such as artificial intelligence, Internet of Things, and telemedicine, hold great promise for improving patient care and operational efficiency in healthcare. However, these technologies also introduce new cybersecurity risks and vulnerabilities that must be addressed to safeguard patient data and protect against cyber threats. Healthcare organizations must embrace innovation while prioritizing security, privacy, and patient safety to harness the benefits of digital transformation while minimizing associated risks.

Ethical considerations, privacy concerns, and patient rights are central to the future of healthcare cybersecurity. Healthcare organizations must uphold ethical standards, respect patient privacy, and ensure patient autonomy and consent in the collection, use, and sharing of health information. By adopting privacy-by-design principles and implementing robust privacy controls, healthcare organizations can build trust and confidence in the healthcare system and empower patients to take control of their health data.

Looking ahead, strengthening healthcare cybersecurity for the future requires a concerted effort from all stakeholders, including healthcare organizations, government agencies, industry partners, and cybersecurity experts. Collaboration, information sharing, and collective action are essential to enhancing cybersecurity defenses, mitigating emerging cyber threats, and safeguarding patient data and safety in an increasingly digitalized healthcare environment.

As we move forward, it is imperative for healthcare organizations to prioritize cybersecurity as a fundamental component of patient care and organizational resilience. Strengthening healthcare cybersecurity requires a multifaceted approach that encompasses technological solutions, policy frameworks, and ethical considerations. Healthcare organizations must invest in cybersecurity awareness and education programs, implement robust security controls and incident response plans, and collaborate with industry partners and regulatory authorities to address emerging cyber threats and ensure the integrity and trustworthiness of healthcare systems and services.

Furthermore, policymakers and regulatory authorities must enact legislation and regulations that promote cybersecurity best practices, incentivize information sharing, and hold healthcare organizations accountable for protecting patient data and mitigating cyber risks. By working together, we can build a more secure and resilient healthcare ecosystem that prioritizes patient privacy, safety, and trust in the digital age.

www.ingramcontent.com/pod-product-compliance
Lightning Source LLC
Chambersburg PA
CBHW050241230526
45470CB00005B/2051